This book is dedicated to:

Marcia Devere, who first told me about the rescue.

Dorothy and Burt Devere, who didn't give up on their horse and told me their story.

Chrystie Devere, who took the photographs on which many of these illustrations are based.

The people of Tombstone, especially Fire Chief Jessie Grassman, Bob "Smokey" Stober, Tombstone High School Principal Robert Devere, and football coach Mike Hayhurst, all of whom worked tirelessly to try and save a horse.

Third edition

PRT1018A

Printed in the United States

Library of Congress Control Number: 2018908416

ISBN: 978-0-578-06346-1

www.mascotbooks.com

STONY'S TALE

A True Tombstone Story

written by

Suzanne M. Malpass

illustrated by

Trish Morgan

Always Be Kind,
Suzanne M. Malpass

EL RANCHO FALTA MAS

"I can't find Stony anywhere," Grandpa Burt said to his wife one boiling hot August day at their Tombstone ranch.

"You know how horses are," said Grandma Dorothy. "He must be somewhere on the hillside. He'll probably show up tomorrow."

But the next day, Stony was still missing. Grandpa Burt set off on his John Deere Gator to find the quarter horse.

After hearing about the missing horse, a neighbor came over and volunteered to search along the fence lines with Grandpa Burt.

When they returned sweaty and tired, the neighbor
shook his head and said to Grandma Dorothy, "We
couldn't find Stony anywhere."

Grandpa Burt added, "And there was no sign that horse
thieves had taken him."

On the third day, Stony was still missing. Grandma Dorothy had to get ready for company, so she and her dog, Miss Patches, walked down the hill toward the guesthouse.

Once they reached the lower ground, Miss Patches started howling. Grandma Dorothy called Grandpa Burt on her cell phone. "I think Miss Patches has found a snake. This is not her usual someone-is-coming bark."

Grandpa Burt made his way slowly down the hill to
check out the area where Miss Patches was still barking.
   He carried a shovel in case she'd found a rattlesnake.
   Grandpa Burt found no rattler but he did find a hole—**a
very deep hole!**

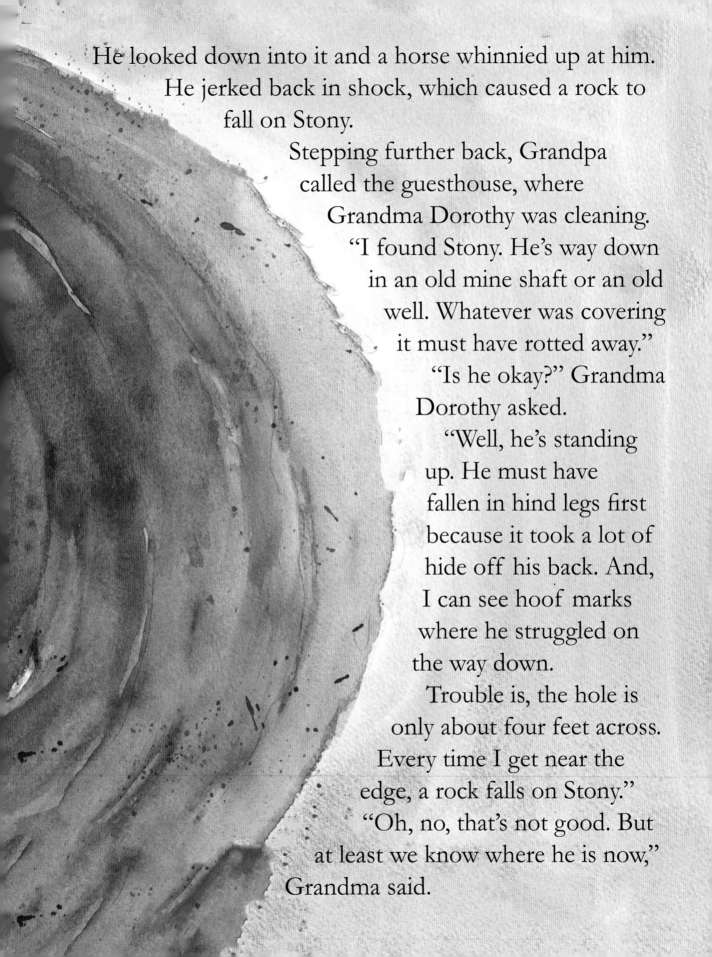

He looked down into it and a horse whinnied up at him. He jerked back in shock, which caused a rock to fall on Stony.

Stepping further back, Grandpa called the guesthouse, where Grandma Dorothy was cleaning. "I found Stony. He's way down in an old mine shaft or an old well. Whatever was covering it must have rotted away."

"Is he okay?" Grandma Dorothy asked.

"Well, he's standing up. He must have fallen in hind legs first because it took a lot of hide off his back. And, I can see hoof marks where he struggled on the way down.

Trouble is, the hole is only about four feet across. Every time I get near the edge, a rock falls on Stony."

"Oh, no, that's not good. But at least we know where he is now," Grandma said.

"I'm going to try the fire department,"
said Grandpa just before he hung up.
When the dispatcher answered, Grandpa
reported, "I'm afraid one of my horses fell down
an old mine shaft or an old well."
Five minutes later the fire chief showed up at the ranch and
headed to where the horse was trapped. Grandpa Burt asked,
"Do you think Smokey might be willing to bring over his front-
end loader so we could try to rescue the poor thing?"
"I was just talking to him at the B.L.M. horse-and-
burro sale," said the chief. "I'll go see if he's still there."

While the fire chief went to talk to Smokey, a neighbor looked down the hole and said, "Just shoot him! You'll never get your horse out of there."

Grandpa Burt bristled. "As long as he's alive, we're sure going to try!"

Soon Smokey arrived with his front-end loader and the fire chief returned with the city's backhoe.

The men started digging a trench. It turned out to be about 50 feet long and angled down to 20 feet deep. It ended right next to the well.

Stony was standing about 8 feet further down, his hindquarters under a ledge of some kind.

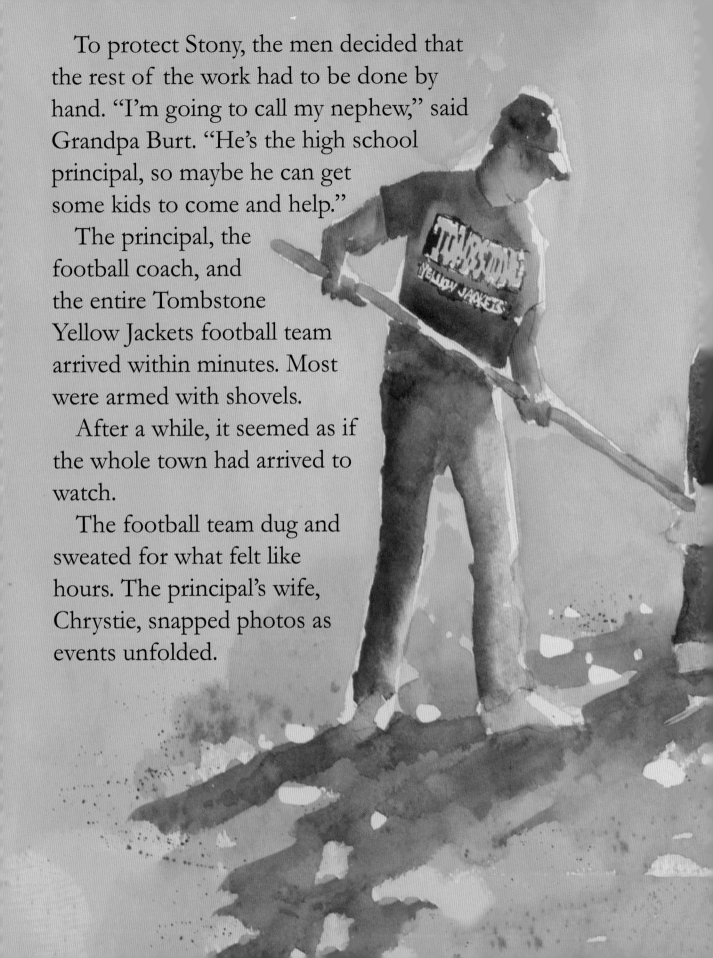

To protect Stony, the men decided that the rest of the work had to be done by hand. "I'm going to call my nephew," said Grandpa Burt. "He's the high school principal, so maybe he can get some kids to come and help."

The principal, the football coach, and the entire Tombstone Yellow Jackets football team arrived within minutes. Most were armed with shovels.

After a while, it seemed as if the whole town had arrived to watch.

The football team dug and sweated for what felt like hours. The principal's wife, Chrystie, snapped photos as events unfolded.

Grandpa Burt paced and worried out loud, "That horse really needs water. But I can't get any to him, with his nose pressed hard up against one wall and his hindquarters under another."

While Grandpa Burt fussed, Stony collapsed. "We've got to get him out!" Grandpa yelled.

The football coach offered, "I've seen horses lifted by the neck. I don't know if it'll kill him, but he's going to die anyway if we don't get him out."

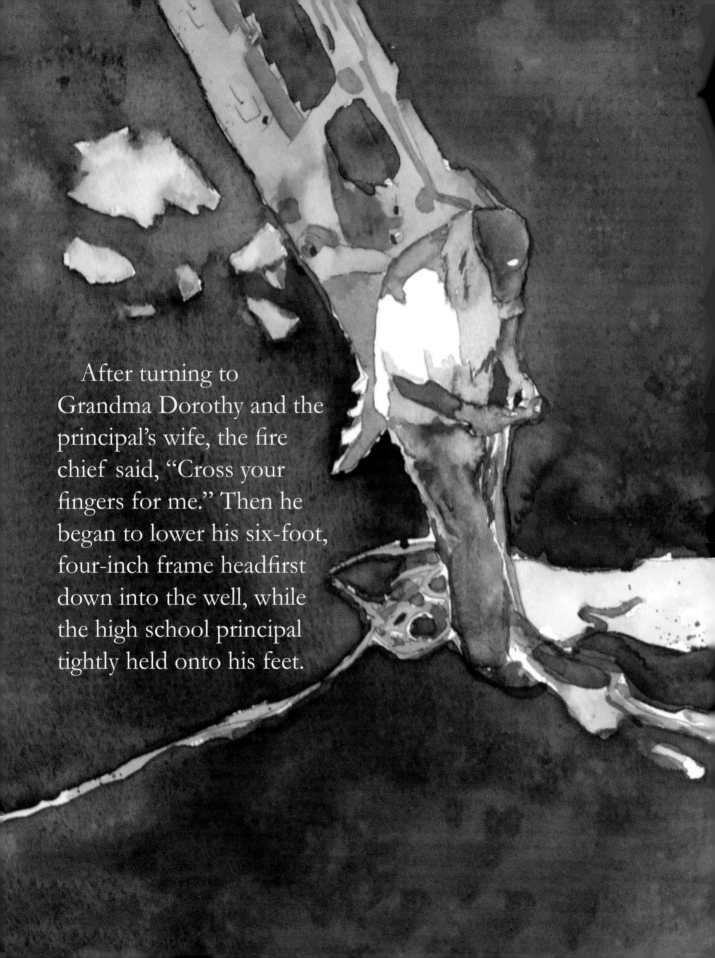

After turning to Grandma Dorothy and the principal's wife, the fire chief said, "Cross your fingers for me." Then he began to lower his six-foot, four-inch frame headfirst down into the well, while the high school principal tightly held onto his feet.

When the crowd saw what the chief was doing, many offered up a silent prayer for his safety. They imagined how dangerous it could be in a confined space with an animal weighing around 1,000 pounds.

The chief managed to hook a halter around Stony's head. He backed out of the hole and climbed onto the backhoe again. He waited as Smokey tied the rope to the backhoe's lifting arm. People held their breath as the backhoe began lifting the horse.

All too soon, the halter broke! Stony was dumped back down the well!

"I can't watch anymore," said Grandma Dorothy. She took off for the house with tears in her eyes.

Someone said, "Maybe this heavy rope would work."

As the principal gripped his feet, the fire chief once again went headfirst back down into the well. The chief secured the rope around Stony's neck and through the rest of the halter.

He crawled back out of the hole and climbed onto the backhoe. Inch by inch, he began to lift Stony again.

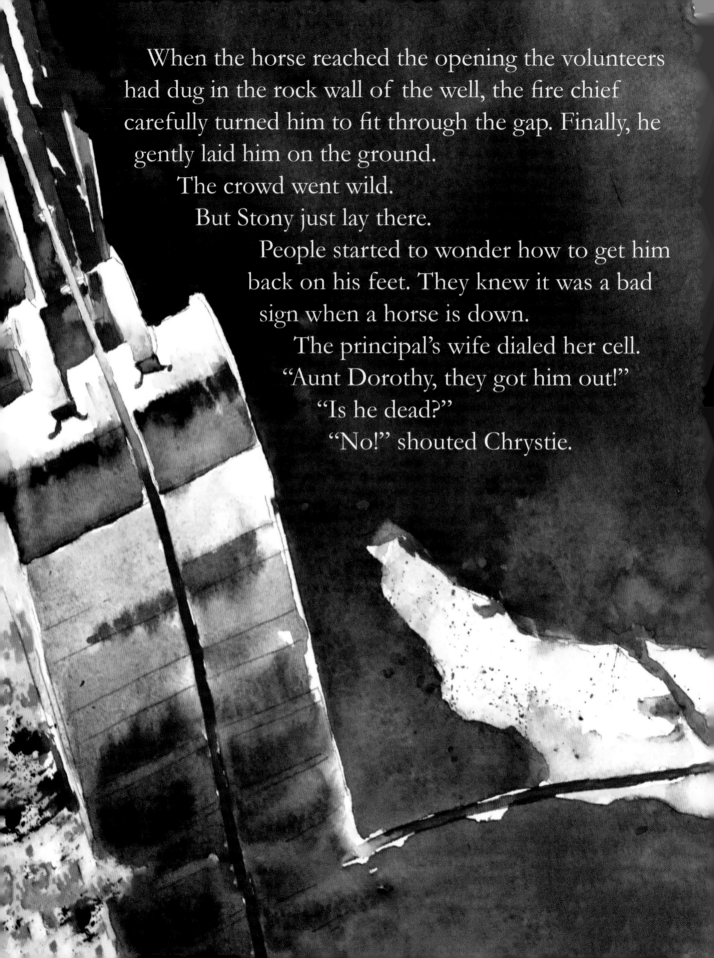

When the horse reached the opening the volunteers had dug in the rock wall of the well, the fire chief carefully turned him to fit through the gap. Finally, he gently laid him on the ground.

The crowd went wild.

But Stony just lay there.

People started to wonder how to get him back on his feet. They knew it was a bad sign when a horse is down.

The principal's wife dialed her cell. "Aunt Dorothy, they got him out!"

"Is he dead?"

"No!" shouted Chrystie.

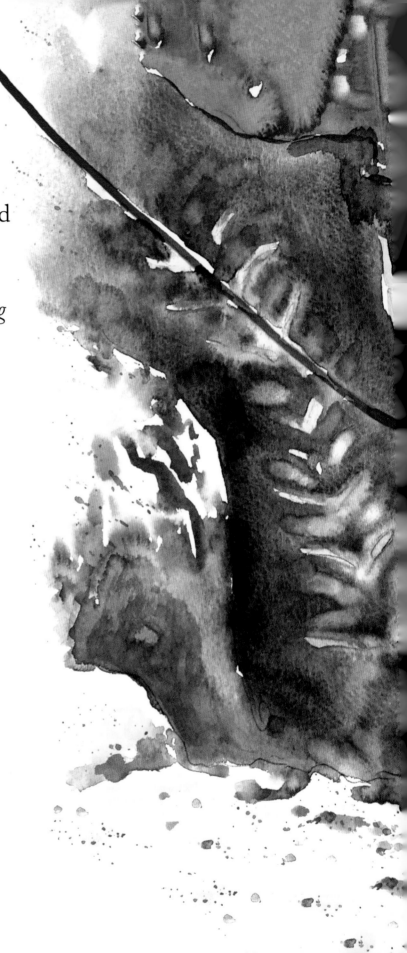

Grandma Dorothy raced back down the hill.

After at least 52 hours down a well and a *loooooong* 30 seconds lying on the ground, Stony stood up. He shook himself off and drank down two five-gallon buckets of water, one right after the other.

Afterwards, Grandpa Burt led his horse away. "Let's wash those sores and put some ointment on them. Then I'll give him a couple shots of antibiotic."

These days Grandma Dorothy, Grandpa Burt, and Stony all live in peaceful retirement at the ranch. Grandpa Burt still likes to tell about Stony's rescue. Even now, he wonders how a horse could fall 28 feet down and not break any bones.

Grandma Dorothy always finishes his story. "Not only did Stony get better physically, he had a change in attitude. In the past when our son, Marc, would ride him, he'd be nice for a while. Then suddenly he'd 'go rodeo' and start to buck. Marc named him after Stony bucked him off on a pile of rocks.

Now Stony is nice all the time."

INTERESTING FACTS

1. Grandpa Burt gave the ranch its Spanish name, El Rancho Falta Mas, meaning "The Ranch that Needs More" or "The Ranch of Many Faults."

2. The B.L.M. stands for the Bureau of Land Management, a federal agency with oversight over countless tracts of land, 99.9% of which are in the West, including Alaska.

3. As an exploration geologist searching for and developing new ore bodies, Grandpa Burt worked at mines in many places in the U.S., as well as in Australia, Canada, Chile, Holland, Indonesia, New Guinea, the Philippines, and Spain.

4. Tombstone, originally called Goose Flats, was incorporated as a city in 1879. Even today, many Tombstone citizens walk around in traditional clothing, which dates from the 1880s.

5. Jessie Grassman is no longer Tombstone Fire Chief.

6. After taking a couple years off, Mike Hayhurst is once again the Tombstone Yellow Jackets' football coach.

7. Former principal, Robert Devere, became the superintendent of Tombstone United School District in June of 2015.

Photograph by Gwen Calhoun

Every year, Suzanne M. Malpass and her husband, Jeff Rogers, spend the summer and fall with their dog, Bonita, in Suzanne's hometown of East Jordan, in northwestern lower Michigan. Each winter and spring, they live in their adopted town of Sierra Vista, in southeastern Arizona.

Other books by Suzanne M. Malpass:

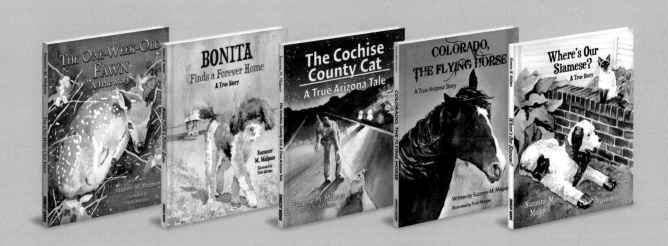